Water Line

by
Jeanne Buesser

2016 © Jeanne Buesser. All rights reserved.
No part of this book may be reproduced, stored in a retrieval system, or transmitted by any means without the written permission of the author.

Books by Jeanne Buesser

He Talks Funny

Moonlight Till Dawn

Journey From Darkness To Light

Willow Tree

Waterline

Acknowledgments

I would like to thank my family and friends for their support especially Andrea, Gwen, Carrie, Naomi. A special shout out to some individuals for all their help with this book. For my art teacher Bobbi, you've helped me grow as an artist. My sons, you've taught me so much and continue to do so. Betty, Lisa and my editors, DC and Cherrye, thank you for all your help in educating me and your support in writing and telling my story. For Dr. Ladak, her caring medical treatment and for writing the professional review. In memory of RJ and Dominick who were special people in my son's life.

Definition of Autism

Autism spectrum disorder is a serious neurodevelopmental disorder that impairs a child's ability to communicate and interact with others.

Autism spectrum disorder (ASD) is a behavior disorder which includes atypical, restricted and repetitive behaviors, interests and activities. These behaviors cause significant impairment in social and communication skills and performance of day to day function.

Children with autism have a wide spectrum of deficits. They have an exceptionally difficult time communicating with others because they lack the ability to use meaningful language in sentences. They may have good memory and might be able to recite favorite phrases from a show or movie repetitively instead of using words or sentences to answer a question.

Their sensory systems are different. Due to this, they exhibit unusual behaviors which include specific food aversions such as handling of flavors or textures. This can include avoiding or not trying new foods, or touching of different foods on a plate. They may avoid certain colored foods or crave for crunchy foods. They have poor orientation in physical and spatial space with others.

Children with autism often manifest poor eye contact and abnormal physical behaviors which hinders them from making friends. They cannot understand and interpret social cues such as the facial expression and tone of voice. Their interaction with children of their own age is inappropriate.

Sometimes they exhibit inappropriate behaviors such as making loud noises, repetitive clapping, finger movements or hand flapping. They are usually very active and cannot keep still.

Autism is a spectrum disorder with wide variation in skill development. children may be delayed in all areas or they can have strong skills in some domains such as reading. The more severely involved children are cognitively impaired and fall in the range of intellectual disability. The children with Autism have a variety of other difficulties such as coordination in standing and walking, toilet training, self-help skills such as dressing and self-feeding.

Children with Autism have short and selective attention. They seem to ignore you when you speak to them and they often do not respond to their name. However, they hear very well and react immediately when you call them for an activity they enjoy such as their favorite TV show.

They seem to be in a fog a great deal of time, yet they can surprise you by their actions as they have specific likes, dislikes and abilities. They are very sensitive and perceive the vibration in their environment, but they may not always show how they feel.

Just because children with autism are atypical and maybe nonverbal it doesn't mean they aren't capable. They just think differently. Given the right support and opportunity, children with Autism will bloom to their best potential.

Forward

My parents grew up during the depression. As a young child, dad had very little and was quite poor. He learned how to adapt and find the skills to survive. My mom too learned how to survive. After they were married, they eventually had a house, three children and a car.

As parents they taught us valuable lessons, such as budgeting and survival mechanism.

My mom was a teacher, which was a favorable thing for me. When I was small, I struggled a lot while studying for tests especially in math.

Things were better for us compared to how my parents' life was. As a family we had a lot of adventures and a lot of support from each other.
I think having that background gave me the strong foundation I needed. I think back about my parents many years ago. The one thing that wasn't talked about in my parents' generation was about emotions or feelings. While growing up, I don't

remember hearing or talking about feelings in the family. We never talked about stuff on an emotional level, yet there was a lot of love and support in our family.
Due to this I didn't do it either. I just learned to do what I needed to do from my mom and approached things in an organized manner.

My mom was the serious one but dad was just the opposite. She the house in order and showed us a lot of strength. My dad worked long hours on a rotating schedule. He was the sort of person who kept to himself, but he was a very gentle and loving person, who loved life. He was a union man and also a person with interesting ideas, beating to his own drum. He always listened but never judged. Always telling stories, jokes, making up poems, or being silly. I am serious like my mom and creative like my dad. At the time, I didn't realize it but I found that later. The one thing that was constant was that they were able to work things out and they loved each other.

Fast forward many years. I grew up, graduated high school and after a few years got married. You can be married to someone for a long time and still not know them well. Feelings and emotions weren't discussed between my husband and myself. Much later I became a mom and that is when things started to change.

About the first rough leg in my journey, I talk about my first born. It is in the forward of my book "He Talks Funny". My other two poetry books are Journey from Darkness to Light and Moonlight till Dawn. These talk about the second part of my journey.

Here I wanted to talk about my relationship with my husband. I can say that when I met my husband our relationship was easy because we were identical in many respect.
My goal in writing this story is to help others understand that children with special needs can achieve things that none of us thought were dreamed possible. This story's timeline is an experience of my younger son (Orien) who is diagnosed with Autism. This is about him from being a young child to growing into his teenage years. This story also shows my older son Marc's timeline. He has Apraxia which is a severe neurological speech disorder. They both have different personalities.

I noticed something was not right with Orien, my youngest son. He often stared into space and did not respond to his name when I called. I called Early Intervention to get him evaluated and they noticed a problem. I took him to see a developmental pediatrician to be diagnosed. I had similar experience previously with Marc. They both have developed different personalities. However, one major difference stands out between my sons.

Marc, my older son is diagnosed with Apraxia. He didn't produce the initial sounds of speech in a word. He never used conversational speech. As a baby and a toddler, he did not babble and his speech pattern consisted of only one sound "mmm" to indicate everything.

Marc presented with low muscle tone in his face, tongue and the abdominal part of his body. He also had a problem in developing a good pencil grip and instead he held the pencil in a fist. He could not keep his coloring within the lines.

Marc understood everything but wasn't able to respond and make sounds. He pointed to objects and would look at me for the word. He had to write the steps as it was harder for him to give the answer. Fortunately, as Marc grew older, at about ten years, he became more social and carried conversations.
My boys are now two high-functioning teenagers even though they have different struggles.

Orien, was diagnosed with autism, at one and a half years of age. He was also assessed for possible seizures. Orien heard and understood what people told him, but he had trouble following directions. As he got older, he could figure out math problems in his head and did not need to write the steps down. Many times he would lie down on the floor refusing to get up. Standing in one place irritated Orien. He liked to run, and he wasn't verbal. Mornings were challenging as he did not want to get up and dress himself.

Since my husband worked many long hours, most of the times, I was in charge of taking care of the children myself. It was a very difficult task as both were non-verbal when they were younger.

Going shopping for food or clothes, was very challenging as Orien wouldn't always stay in the cart, or allow me to hold his hand. Loud noises really affected him and he would cover his ears or backed away.

Raising my sons was difficult at times as whenever we were in public places not everyone understood their behavior. This was frustrating for me. If I was lucky, I was able to get a few food items, before he would have a tantrum in the store. People couldn't understand what I was going through and they stared, while he tossed around.

He had many sensory symptoms. Tags on clothes were a problem. They would itch a lot and had to be removed. Sometimes it was the texture or the color of the clothes. It often became a very stressful situation.

While I was thinking about this story, I thought Orien should write something in it.

At age 12, Orien wrote a small paragraph in his own words on this page. This is a swimming story. This paragraph is written through Orien's eyes. I asked my son to write in his own words what it feels like learning how to swim. His teachers helped to put his thoughts together.

How I Felt When I Learned to Swim
by Orien

This summer I learned how to swim at Graydon Pool in Ridgewood. I would go every Monday morning to a swimming class lesson. My swimming teacher was a man with brown hair. The 1st time I learned the breaststroke, I was so happy!

I smiled all day!

I had a green bathing suit! I showed mom my new swimming moves. I loved to wear my US divers goggles when I swim. I lost my goggles at the Ridgefield pool this summer. I hope next summer I will get a new pair of goggles and flippers.

They will make me swim fast! I would love that.

Swimming requires a lot of practice and time. But first a great coach who can guide you and help you learn your swimming strokes and kicks. You have to be able to understand instructions and listen.

The swimmer has to want to learn and needs to learn how to breathe underwater and shallow dive. There are many stokes that you can learn and the kicks that go along with them. Having the swim goggles, swim caps, and proper swim suits helps. Australian crawl (freestyle), side stroke, breast stroke, backstroke, butterfly.

My children always teach me so much. I have learned how to be more patient and not to have any expectations from them while they were growing up. Even if it took a long time for me to see the results, they have come a long way and I am a proud mom. That's were my patience came in handy.

As I am writing this story, I suddenly realize that it is also therapeutic for me as I am diving from the platform into life.

Jeanne Buesser

Waterline

SUMMER OF 2004

Edward, my husband, worked long hours so he wasn't always available to go to the town pool with us. But today it was different. When he announced he was going to join us, I was relieved to know I have help and the children were also so happy to have their dad. Most of the times I would be doing this by myself.

I scurried about getting everything ready for the pool just as I always did but I wondered if Orien would pose a problem. I asked myself "Would he have one of his meltdowns before even getting to the car or while we were in the car?"

It was a big relief to know I had help because it was always hard for me to lift the boys out of the water. Since Orien loved the pool so much, Edward would be at hand to help me drag him out, if needed. Today I had help!

The whole Starze family arrived at the town pool on a hot scorching day in July. The sun beamed down on our heads There was also a playground near the pool.

Surprisingly, the tall wrought iron gates that secured the pool were locked. With our swimming gear in full haul, we waited patiently for the attendant to open the gates.

The boys loved the water just as much as Edward did. As soon as the attendant opened the gates, both the boys plunged forward nearly knocking her down. I was a little embarrassed, but I managed to smile at the young lady. She smiled back and so I was relieved.

Edward had just as much fun as the boys. Before I knew it, there was a loud splash. The water was now on the sides of the pool. Edward tossed the boys around in the pool while I sat and enjoyed the scene. Both boys giggled with joy at the prospect of another toss from their Dad.

Many times, I waited outside while my sons changed into bathing suits, hoping they wouldn't fight, play inside, or fall in bathrooms. Quite often I would get strange looks from people in the community who didn't understand what children with special needs are like. Many times I was anxious and unable to relax by the pool, unlike other mothers, since the boys are physically bigger than I was.

In my heart I prayed Orien would interact with others, sharing the sandbox and playing on the swings or slides. Instead, Orien would run so fast without saying anything, I couldn't catch him when he took off. I was glad to see them having so much fun, but deep inside I worried since neither of the boys swam well. I began to realize that physically I wouldn't be able to get them out of the pool safely, in case something happened. I wanted them to be safe in the pool. I wanted them to learn to swim well and not be at risk. Sometimes I was afraid that they wouldn't be allowed to go to the pool anymore as people didn't understand Orien's behavior including the lifeguards.

"How could I find a swim teacher for the boys?" I thought to myself. It would be very hard to teach because both boys had a problem of listening carefully and to follow instructions. I thought to myself, If I found the right teacher, the boys could have fun while they practiced swimming and followed safety rules.

I asked the lifeguards at the pool and I even asked around, but I didn't have much luck. It was quite frustrating. I learned about some lifeguards who had worked with children who didn't always listen.

Since Marc was older, and didn't have the same behaviors that Orien did, Marc started taking lessons at the local pool. The swim class was large and comprised of different ages of "noisy" children.

Many other kids who didn't take lessons would also jump in from the side of the pool near where they practiced. This became a lot of struggle for Marc. Free swim times and swim lessons ran concurrently. Marc tried to keep his head above the water and not turn his head too much to keep water from splashing on his face. However, Mark did not receive the attention he needed.

I began to ask around but didn't get many answers. So I looked up in the local phonebooks and newspapers in the library. I also researched online for swimming lessons for children with special needs in my area. Luck was on my side, as I found one place which only had group lessons and times. However, it didn't work out for me and the boys. The cost was also very high.

Success came when I found Young Jewish Community Center of Bergen County, which offered individualized lessons that fit my schedule and budget.

There were women coaches trained in CPR who worked with a swim team. I learnt about coaches for a special needs swim team for Marc and signed him up for the class there. Marc tried out for the Special Olympics Swim Team, and success came to Marc. He learned about different strokes, kicks and how to use all his muscles.

I asked a lot of questions to the coach about swimming rules, meets, strokes, dives, flips etc. I listened and learnt from the woman coach. The coach continued, "There can be as many as six swimmers in a heat (race) at one time." "Swimmers can earn ribbons or medals, from 1st to 6th place in the special swim meets. There are rules too on how to swim properly and things you shouldn't do." "You have to remember to touch the wall when you've finished the race, and not stand at the bottom of the pool. You can get disqualified." "Good swimmers learn not to take too many breaths because it slows down their swimming strokes." Every other Sunday, Edward my husband took Marc to the swim practices, where he would meet and talk to the other parents and Marc's teammates.

I would take Orien to speech therapy so I wasn't able to go to all the swimming practices with Marc.

Marc did well and earned many ribbons and medals. He swam against many different swimmers from diverse geographic areas. He competed at the state level and continued to win medals as he advanced.

As Orien got older, it was time for him to enroll in swim lessons at the local pool. However, he didn't cooperate with the other kids or the swim coach there. So I started him on private lessons at the place where Marc practiced. I made sure the boys took practice lessons at different times.

I wasn't sure if I would be allowed to watch Orien in the pool area or If I would distract him. I wondered about how Orien would fare. I was quite anxious. But the swim coaches knew what to do. Orien had a helper in the pool to keep him focused on his strokes.
He learned how to stay still and wait until he was called. Reports from the coaches showed progress as Orien swam half the length of the pool!

Marc, the older brother grew stronger and leaner as he practiced and he began to swim faster. Breathing underwater was hard as he had to coordinate between moving his arms and kicking his feet. He became quite confident and accomplished. At one meet, right from the start, he shot out of the water like a rocket.

Sometimes Orien came along to the swim meets with me. In turn they provided much valued support to each other. Orien's body was much smaller and not as muscular as Marc's but he was active. It was hard for Marc to swim during practice when Orien was around. Orien would jump in and out of the water while Mark was trying to practice. Marc had been swimming for three years now. I found myself yelling, my voice becoming hoarse when the team swam at the meets. I took pictures and videos and my heart swelled with pride. When Orien got a little older, I started a new part time job at a school.

Orien began to understand the directions. He started doing well and his abilities improved day by day. I enquired from the coach if he could be on the same team as Marc. To this the coach agreed to take him on.

Then came the difficult part and things changed…Marc decided he didn't want to swim any longer and didn't want his brother on the team! The coaches tried very hard and talked to him to be on the team. However, Mark had made up his mind. He wanted to be on a different team but there wasn't any available.

Then things changed from bad to much worse… How things can change in life in a second….

That day I came home early from work. I found that my husband Edward had passed away. I was very shocked and hurt. Fifteen years earlier, I had to cope with the loss of my first child.

I went into survival mode.

I began doing what I knew had to be done. I called family members, teachers and swim coaches while trying to hold myself together.

Everyone responded quickly. Orien was getting off the bus. I knew I had to get Marc from his after school activity. I drove there silently but my stomach was in knots. "How was I going to tell them?" It hit me really hard. A wave of a long buried emotional feeling rose up again inside me. It was not having any control, reeling into the darkness like a spiral. This was the same feeling I had many years ago. Scrambling, I was all alone now.

I anguished over raising my children alone without any backup or guide. My brain froze, my body was shaking and tears streamed down my cheeks. My legs and body felt like jelly.

Things are very different now. Everything is changed. My bed is empty. Now the boys and I had to adjust to a new life without their dad. Marc and Orien couldn't talk about their dad. They went to Art Grief Therapy sessions where the boys talked and expressed their feelings by drawing pictures. They went there for many months. I also went to see a counselor. I was devastated trying to hold everything together for my new family.

The days and nights went by very slowly for everyone.

Marc and Orien didn't know how to talk about their memories of their dad. Some of the swim team's dads helped with Orien while I waited for Orien to get changed at swimming practice. That really helped even though it was bitter sweet. Prior to that I had to take him into the women's room to change and that didn't go well as he got older.

One day, Orien, Marc, myself and the coach were walking down the hall after swim practice. Orien was very quiet and stopped walking. Suddenly he burst into tears without a warning. "What's wrong, Orien?" I stopped and asked, running to his side. "I MISS DADDY!" he sobbed, tears running down his face. That happened to be the first complete sentence he said out loud by himself. Usually he would repeat his favorite phrases instead of speaking in full sentences. I held him close and kissed his head. My heart broke as I tried to assure Orien things would be okay, but I couldn't take away their pain.

Marc replied, "Orien, dad will always be in your heart", putting his arm around his little brother's shoulders. As they walked towards the door, the coach had tears in her eyes.

Over the summer, Orien had grown taller and stronger. He was now almost the same height as Mark. The team had been practicing their strokes and learning how to jump and dive from the starting block into the water. The first county meet was coming up soon. The coach asked if Orien had ever been taught the stroke for the butterfly? "No Why? I asked?" "He tried doing it today by himself during the pool practice," the coach exclaimed! "Really?" I replied, "He must have been watching Marc's heat." "He is diving so far out from the starting block, that he is near the finishing rope" the coach informed me.

An excited Orien looked forward to his first meet. He packed goggles, swim suit, flip flops, towels, swim shirt and swim cap in his duffle bag the night before. Orien, Marc and I woke up early, bringing the gym bag along with a camera, and our lunches. We all piled into the car and drove away. Marc helped Orien find the changing room near the pool. Orien changed very quickly on his own and found the coach and his team. He was maturing so quickly.

His swimmer ID number was written on his arm along with the numbers of his heat events. Parents and friends sat waiting on the carpeted but uncomfortable concrete steps. Humidity and strong chlorine smell permeated the pool area. Different teams walked proudly around the pool. Everyone cheered as they were announced. The national anthem played and everyone stood up. After saying the Pledge of Allegiance, they sat down. I cheered the whole team as they swam. Orien watched the competing swimmers and waited patiently for his turn to swim in the pool area. That is a lot of effort and work for Orien including not touching anyone. The coach had worked with the whole team to keep their hands to themselves, and not to make noises.

Finally, his turn came. Orien stood on the blocks. Other swimmers rested in the water or stood on the blocks awaiting the signal to dive in. At the sound of the horn, they all dived in. Orien pushed hard from the starting block with his legs and arms and flew into the water... I took out my camera and waited... I was yelling "Pull! Pull! Pull! Go Sharks!!" My voice cracked. No more sounds emerged from my hoarse throat. I heard Marc's familiar voice yelling next to me, "Come on you can do it, Orien, Pull!" I smiled and was proud to see how Marc continued cheering for his younger brother. In the past Orien had watched Marc swim and he took it all in but, he was nonverbal. Volunteers gave pieces of paper by age and rank to the coaches after each race. Orien sat down waiting for the volunteers to tally up the stop watch times.

As the Olympic Anthem played Orien stood up and walked to the steps. These showed their performance numbers written on them. The numbers ranged from 1st place through 6th place. Orien forgot to touch the wall with both hands, so he was disqualified. He got a ribbon for trying and he smiled.

The next big swim meet was with swimmers from other larger areas. Orien was very excited and seemed ready again for the challenge. His aunt came from Connecticut to watch and sat with Marc and me. Orien posed on the platform and stepped onto the diving blocks. "What heat was he in," Marc asked. "Thirty or thirty-one?" "Thirty-one," I replied, and looked at the program.

Orien stood on the blocks and he dived into the pool. "Oh, no he has jumped in the wrong heat!" Marc shouted. Orien now competed with much older people! He didn't wait, he went ahead.

Orien swam so fast no one knew what had happened! He went to the end of the pool and touched the wall with both hands. His hands flew up with his fists in the air. He was excited and happy. Once out of the pool, Orien was handed a piece of paper by the volunteers. The paper had his swim ranking on it. He held it up as he was walked to the seats and waited with the other swimmers with his towel. Neither his aunt or I could see the number from where we were sitting in the stand.

At last, his heat number was called. He went by the platform with the group of swimmers and waited. The Olympic anthem played as he stepped onto the ranking blocks. I ran to see the ranking blocks. He had proudly held up a white piece of paper, with a number one written on it! Orien won the gold medal. 1St place!

Orien was so proud of himself and grinned from ear to hear. I hurried and dashed over to the platform to snap a picture and give him a high five!

Marc, his aunt and I were very proud and happy. Orien had won a medal against swimmers bigger than him. We the family didn't know that was ever possible!

You never know until you try!

Prologue

Today, Orien still swims on the team and wins medals and ribbons for his progress. Marc and Orien are both on a regular bowling team, receiving trophies and having fun.

Resources

artsmendshearts@gmail.com
201-280-8880
Susan Greif
Creative Arts Therapy Consultant

Laura Hudson, MS, ATR-BC, LCAT
Director/Art Therapist
Hearts & Crafts Grief Counseling
330 B Broadway
Hillsdale, NJ 07642
201-818-9399
www.heartsandcraftscounseling.org

Academy of Country Music: Lifting Lives
The charitable arm of the Academy of Country Music, which supports a variety of charitable organizations that improves lives through the power of music.

Advantage Speech & Language Services

ARC Assoc and equity for underserved student

"Author aims to educate public about autism spectrum"

Article on Jeanne by Kelly Nicholaides of the South Bergenite

The Cherab Foundation (also on Facebook)

The Cherab Foundation is a world-wide nonprofit organization working to improve the communication skills and education of all children with speech and language delays and disorders

Double Rainbow
Mission Statement: "To offer genuine respect to people with special needs for their individual uniqueness."

LD Online
The world's leading website on learning disabilities and ADHD

The Little Gym

Parents' Point of View- Jeanne's new blog on jeannebuesser.com website

Asperger Syndrome Education Network- website aspennj.org

New Jersey Self-Help Clearing House
New Jersey Speech and Hearing
A wonderful site for parents/professionals with resources/conferences info

http://www.autismontheseas.com/
Cruises for special needs families
Eastersealsnj.org
www.eastersealsnj.org
http://specialeducationalliancenj.org/
AFSNJ Northern Regional Office
322 US Hwy 46, Suite 290,
Parsippany, NJ 07054

Autism of New Jersey
500 Horizon Drive, Suite 530
Robbinsville, NJ 08691
800-428-8476
Website: njcosac.org

The Autism Society
4340 Ease-West Hwy, Suite 350
Bethesda, MD 20814
autism-society.org
800-328-8476

Autism Self Advocacy Network
PO Box 66122
Washington, DC 20035
(202) 596-1056
website autisticadvocacy.org

http://www.autismlink.com/dir/cosac-new-jersey-center-for-outreach
and-services for the-autism-community/

Autism Family Services of New Jersey
1 AAA Drive, Suite 203
Website autismfamilyservicesnj.org
Telephone 877-237-4477

www.easterseals.org
www.sonj.org

Special Needs:
www.americaspecialkidz.org
www.specialeducationalliancenj.org
www.nutritionwithapurpose.us

Chaye lamm warburg- OT
www.potsot.com/workshops

Nutrition with a purpose- Tommy Dalton
973-295-2134
www.nutritionwithapurpose.us

Moms Support Group
www.mom2momus.com
1-877-914-6662

http://www.abcmusicandme.com/special-needs.html

www.massport.com/logan-airport/about-logan/Airport%20Programs/WingsforAutism.aspx

http://www.spicelandsriding.com/

Dolphinquest.com

Research:

http://www.abcmusicandme.com/research.html

Alignment with the standards;
http://blog.abcmusicandme.com/wp-content/uploads/LL_To_CCSS_Correlation_Chart1.pdf

www.aquinasspecialneeds.com

Asperger Syndrome Education Network
9 Aspen Circle
Edison, NJ 08820
Website: aspennj.org
Telephone: (732) 321-0880

http://www.opencollegesgroup.com.au/
Education, support and advocacy on issues dealing with spectrum disorders.

www.aquinasspecialneeds.com

www.teachkids.kindermusik.net-for families (my classes/schedule/offerings)
www.healthline.com/health/developmental-coordination-disorder
NICHCY
National Youth Organization more great articles on Apraxia
Say it with Symbols! (also on Facebook)
Resource for families, caregivers, educators and therapists who help children and adults with communication challenges communicate and gain independence using augmentative communication (AAC) and visual supports with symbols and pictures.

"Speaking loudly on talking 'funny'"
Bryan Wassal of NorthJersey.com interviews Jeanne about her book.

www.brainandspinalcord.org/cerebral-palsy/types/erbs-palsy.html
http://nursinghomeabuseguide.com/